CONTE

Poetry
Cheese

Edited by Tim Harrison

**With some words of
encouragement by Roger McGough**

cH
cornerHOUSE Books

Published by
cornerHOUSE Books
26 Effingham Road
Surbiton KT6 5JY

First published 2018

David Loffman's poetry published courtesy of
conjuringsunlight.blogspot.com

Della Reynolds' poetry published courtesy of
poetinpyjamas.com

Morris Thain's poem first appeared in **The Good Life**
newspaper, and is reprinted by kind permission

Snow Bird by Frances White first appeared in **Swiftscape**, by
Frances White (The Seventh Quarry Press, 2017)

Horse by Frances White first appeared in **Away with Words, An
Anthology of Poetry** by Aeronwy Thomas, Annie Taylor, Beryl
Myers and Frances White (Poetry Monthly Press, 2007)

If this little volume has inspired you to come along to a poetry
workshop or a poetry evening at the cornerHOUSE (either
to share original works, or simply listen), and enjoy a hearty
cheese supper, check future dates at **www.thecornerhouse.org**

No animals were harmed in the making of this book

ISBN 978-1-9993575-0-4

Printed and bound in Great Britain by Direct Colour, Unit 1,
Chessington Trade Park, 60 Cox Lane, Chessington KT9 1TW

Cover picture: David Loffman declaims as Tim Harrison sits, enthralled

INTRODUCTION

It all began on Friday June 10 2016, with an 'informal evening of verse' in the studio space of the cornerHOUSE, the community arts centre at 116 Douglas Road, Surbiton. Alerted by word of mouth, email and a Good Life article headlined *Poetry evening? It could be verse*, 40 people turned up to listen to, or read, lines composed on the themes of relationships, stormy weather and food.

Co-ordinated by Nicky Newberry and Ian Davies, the evening featured an extensive cheeseboard, plus accompanying biscuits, olives, gherkins and cherry tomatoes, set out on a trestle table in the foyer. The cheese supper was included in the £4 entry price, and at 7pm the arts centre's bar staff began pouring the wine and beer – seemingly the essential lubricants to poetry.

As the start time of 8pm neared, the circular tables (each with a lit candle) began filling in the Rocard Room. I sat on stage in a snug orange chair, summoning poets by topic to deliver their lines from a lectern. The template was set.

Since then there have been a string of Friday night poetry evenings, preceded by workshops led by David Loffman – the first on an afternoon in April 2017.

Themes for poetry have included remembrance, mirrors, trees, recipes, rivers, animals, rhythm, windows, rain, spring, solitude, revolution and science.

Confidence among Surbiton's pool of poets has steadily risen, and lines once hesitantly muttered are now recited with belief and conviction.

However, few come close to Loffman's own skilfully paced delivery as he stands in the spotlight, supported by his trademark stick. This versifying tripod holds the audience's attention like no other.

Over two and a half years the cheese selection has become bolder as Ian Davies plunders the deeper recesses of Sainsbury's chilled cabinets, although brie and the garlic-flavoured roulé still seem to be the favourites of the cognoscenti.

In a spin-off evening in October 2018, artist Roger Fowler staged an exhibition of his animal drawings and paintings, accompanied by themed poetry readings from cornerHOUSE bards.

The verse shows no sign of drying up. This little volume gives a taste of some of the original works inspired by, and read aloud at, the cornerHOUSE poetry evenings. Special thanks to Nicky Newberry for tirelessly pursuing contributors for their offerings. 'Herding poets' could become a new idiom for a challenging task.

I invited Roger McGough to contribute a few words of support to our first book, which is entitled *Poetry Cheese* to echo his Radio 4 programme *Poetry Please*. I'd interviewed him for a magazine feature back in 2006 to coincide with the paperback launch of *Said and Done*, his soul-baring autobiography.

"Don't ring him before 12," his publicist had instructed. "He'll be running round Barnes Pond until then!" McGough told me he was a creature of routine, with regular rituals. "Each day I go into my study, sit there and start fiddling," he said.

His advice is to have multiple works in progress, to be finished as moods dictate. "Peter Blake has six or seven paintings on the go at any one time," he explained, adding that he intended to carry on writing poetry "until I haven't any new ones".

Tim Harrison

McGough

I wanted to write like
Roger McGough

Tiny words
Clever laughs
A big heart

Sadly

He is a genius
I am

Not

Ian Davies

SOME WORDS OF ENCOURAGEMENT
FROM ROGER McGOUGH

The more poems you start to write

The more poems you have to finish.

Good luck to all you poets in Tolworth!

Best wishes

Roger McGough

(Now off round the pond I joggle)

EMMENTAL

Renewal

The crunch of the gravel,
the rot of the apple,
the droop of the hebe,
the curl of the fern.
The moss on the carpet
between rows of raspberries –
each day makes a difference,
each dies in its turn.

The crunch of the gravel,
the rain on the ivy,
the feverfew dancing,
each blade and each leaf
spends all summer struggling
and autumn receding
and death visits each in
the night like a thief.

The crunch of the gravel,
the redness of apple,
the streak of the mallow,
the camomile mound.
The rose in its glory,

its petals so perfect,
will wither, turn umber,
return to the ground.

Each tiny green seedpod
will burst and drop presents,
each clover curl up soon
and fall in decay.
Each new life will hasten
and greet days of springtime,
push leaf mould aside and
burst up through the clay.

The garden is dying,
the garden is living.
Life passes away and
life wakens anew.
Each seed is a moment,
each seed is a lifetime –
it goes on and on and
it passes on through.

Gill Davies

Spring Awakening

Cold clouds shroud the sun's weak light
Casting filmy shadows on the chilled damp loam
Where silent cells divide and swell and surge
Before the knotted sweat of summer crashes home.
The bruised land shifts its scrawny limbs
To feel the shock of life push past the clammy shield
Empty chambers fill and burst
Breaking the crust the cold has seared and sealed.
Altered states of seed and spore
Tunnel like moles to meet the blinding light
Shift and push and shift again
Gathering strength to shove and win the fight.
What are we, here in winter's wake?
Survivors listening for the distant dance
The tempo steady as a pagan pulse.
Drumbeats waiting for the moment to advance.

Hilary Walker

Gathering of Waters

On the earth sponge
a fall of water
heavy on the mountain shoulder.

Rock locked in cloud,
fusing in blindness,
cradled in turf
till the great
weight of water
forces the turf apart.

No vague direction,
no casual movement
but the one downward plunge
to the planet's centre.

Then the splintering of water on rock
Catches light in its descent,
spilling over mountain lips
that cannot contain
the water flow.

I came to witness
a gathering of waters,
the towering sound
spiralling out of the trap of rock,
patches of light
stretched across the mountains back,
water and rock entwined.

David Loffman

Autumn Throng

Toasted russets, titian golds,
Lie shrivelled and worn
Spiralling on their final journey
from lawn to lawn

Crossing busy roads
In packs of tens
Hobbling crab like on
Pincer ends

A sea of orangey browns
brutally crushed
By heavy feet
And the occasional
squeals of fun.

Paula Scott

Poetry Evening

New Poetry on themes of
Food | Stormy Weather | Relationships
Readers welcome

Friday June 10
7.30pm for 8pm
Tickets £4 (includes cheese & biscuits)
Bookings & information: info@thecornerhouse.org
www.thech.org
corner COMMUNITY
HOUSE ARTS 116 Douglas Road Surbiton KT6 7SB

Silver Birches

I grew up in a house called Silver Birches.
A comfortable middle-class name, I suppose, but we were a comfortable
middle-class sort of family and there were, after all, silver birches in the garden.

Tall, elegant trees, leaves a bit too small perhaps,
like delicate, slender fingers on a grown man.
And branches that began far above the ground,
too high for climbing, even for wiry, bony-legged boys
with little sense of danger,
and trunks that were smooth and rough simultaneously;
unassailable.

But it was the seeds that clamoured for attention,
the mad profusion of nature,
a million cast to the wind that one or two may grow.
Minuscule alongside a conker, an acorn even.

Everywhere we found them,
tiny flying saucers that made their way into books, bedding, bath.
And their seed-companions, tiny aeroplanes
like the ones dad flew in the war (to my boyish eye)
piling up in crashed squadrons in a doorway or garage corner,
suspended mid-flight in a spider's web,
or attached, limpet-like, to my socks.

Silver birches, companions of my childhood, there before I was born,
there when I left home, there still perhaps, longer-lived than I'll be.
We blossom and flourish as leaves on the tree
And wither and perish…
But we are trees, not leaves.
We mark the seasons as they come and go,
rake the dead leaves and see their successors unfurl, sooner or later to see them fall.

And now, at the foot of my garden again there are silver birches,
though the house this time is called, prosaically, 20A.
But still the seeds go everywhere.

Simon Hancock

BRIE ON RYE: APPENZELLER, ÉPOISSES... AND EWE

Horse

After an uphill climb, we rest awhile
beneath the cool dark pine.
Sweetly shaded leisure time
wishing this hired horse were mine.

Frances White

Summer of Hoofs and Manes

The child and the horse ran together
Through fields of sparkling corn.
Two golden manes flashed in time.
A snort, a whinny, a giggle a yell
Was all that could be heard
Throughout those endless summers.

Now the horse is gone to heavenly
fields
And I am grown old with a greying
mane

And the sweet, sweet freedom
Of those childhood days
Is but a memory that comes to
haunt me
When the nights are long…

A hoof and a mane
Long ago, yet clear, so clear
Filling these poor fading eyes
With a tear and a tear and a tear…

Alice Maslen

Companion

In bed, off school, another cold
Downstairs in the distance my mother sings to the housework
and I lie with my book, and sniff
and doze
and cough.
Then he's here, my cat,
jumping up, padding around, palpating my legs beneath the counterpane
in search of the comfortable fold.
Now his claws pierce the covers, and with a yell I throw him off;
but soon he's back. Is that contrition in those green eyes?
  – sorry I hurt you, won't do it again.
He purrs, arches his back to the stroke of my too-warm hand
and settles contentedly;
his idling-engine sound subsides to the soft breath of sleep.
Does he care about me? Of all the beds in the house he has chosen mine
so I tell myself he does.
The day trickles by in elongated hours
but he's still with me, my faithful sick visitor.
I never did the same for him.

Simon Hancock

Heron Redux

The mist lifts on the Barge Walk by the Thames,
And there he is, on a gravel beach.
Disturbed, he clatters off on noisy wings,
Then, effortless, he sweeps right up the reach.

A silent fisherman, who stands and waits,
More come, each year, down river, lock and weir
On wide grey wings, to nest suburban aits.
No longer quite as shy as they once were.

The urban heron has become streetwise,
Or is that riverwise? He hangs around
On roof tops watching with his beady eyes
To steal the goldfish in your garden pond.

The water pure again, in white-grey pairs
They're back to claim the river which was theirs.

Graham Parker

Cat got sick

Cat got sick
Went to vet
Blood test cost
Arm and leg
Dicky thyroid
Too much hormone
Needed pills
Every morning
Cat got hungry
Ate the food
Put on weight
Better mood
Stopped her crying
In the night
Wish I could
Put myself right
First I'm hot
Then I'm cold
Hormone fading
Getting old
She has too much
I've too little
Shame we can't
Meet in the middle.

Della Reynolds

Sleepy Sheep

A field full of sleepy sheep.
Compelled, they leap
over the low point in the fence.
Exhausted, they huddle
in the next field.

Suddenly their route is reversed.
They force-fly back
into their first field.

A grumpy shepherd
counts each crossing the divide.
His eyes droop
but he keeps on
his accounting task.
The sheep resent
being kept awake.

The shepherd longs for release.
Of course, the sheep are safe for
the night in either field.
The shepherd
is tired and witless;
his task is pointless.

Ian Davies

A Horse's Eye

He winked at me. A long, languid wink
And I marvelled at the world of wisdom in a horse's eye.

Nut-brown and knowing, it watched me.
I stared into that deep pool, and there we stood.

Lashes to lashes, trust to trust.

Tim Harrison

Snow Bird

Breasting the blizzard
she swirls
through veils of light
to the shoreline

Where he unhooks
his catch
holds out whiting
on raw hands.
She hovers over
the slippery meat
feathers warm
in the harsh air.

Too cold
to speak or follow
he watches her circle
once around
The shingle beach
to vanish gladly
on bitter wind
fresh fish in her belly.

Frances White

London Horses

High and haughty
Striking poses
The tall bronze horses
Of square and corner
Carry their burdens
Of Dukes and Generals
With pride and honour.

As the men of battle
Of plain and field
Hold high their swords
Of gleaming steel,
Their bold bronze horses
With rounded hooves
Beat the drum
Of the thick London air.

But…
What of those horses
Of flesh and feeling?
Who died in those battles
In pain and panic
And noise and horror?
Those bronze beauties
Chose not to remember
And, like their Generals,
Condemn and ignore.

Philippa Alexander

Wall Jumpers

"Damned wall jumpers in Top Pasture!"
He'd noted they weren't all his sheep
and went back after supper
to sort them out.
No moon, his boots sunk
as he leant into the lower slopes
behind the farmhouse.

He climbed over gate and stile, calling
"Here Meg".
The collie circled the perimeter, sniffing
for treats of afterbirth. In the silence
new lambs were being born
steaming on the cold hillside
to survive or not
he wouldn't know till dawn
but now
he was tracking trespassers.

No sign, till he reached a sheltered hollow
by the last gate onto open fell
and startled a band of ewes.
They thundered in an avalanche over limestone rocks
the white outcrop just discernible.
He'd missed cornering them and cursed
striding down the slope, shouting for the dog.
"To heel! Come in a hint!"
They bolted this way and that, frantic
to escape the collie, as she darted
through the dark and crouched, panting.

Stones tumbled when they breached the wall.
He followed through and set to, rebuilding
securing his boundary with fallen slabs
blocking the way he'd come. He knew
another way back, steeper, more slippery
so pitch black, he couldn't see his feet.

"That was a tricky one, eh Meg?
And a torch would've been a good idea."

Frances White

A Singular Animal

The animals came in two by two,
The sheep, the deer, the kangaroo
Then, lumbering in, a bull and moo,
A brace of pheasants, lizards too,
And Noah watched, and ticked them off,
Two tall giraffe (one with a cough).
The peace was briefly cut to smidgens
Japheth's cat was at the pigeons!

Soon the twinfold tide resumed;
A pair of horses, both well groomed.
Shem and Ham became distracted
(Loading beasts could be protracted),
Eagles, oysters, oxen, goats,
At this rate we might need two boats.
The buffalo, and still they came,
Two insects… I forget their name.

Two ducks, two rabbits, caribou…
Then Noah spotted something new.
'Oi, Ham, just what on earth is that?'
He asked the son he'd first begat
'I think I saw one round at Daniel's
'That thing there, between the spaniels.'
'Really this just will not do,'
Said Noah, and he stopped the queue.

'There's only one of it, thank God,
But in itself that's rather odd.'
A label hung from round its neck
So Shem examined it. 'By 'eck!
'A cockapoo? Now, what's that, dad?'
'I've no idea,' he told the lad.
So Noah, he reviewed his list
But 'cockapoo', that name was missed.

'It's poodle-like,' said Ham to help.
The cockapoo let out a yelp
Then wagged its tail as if to say
'You're half-right, that's my mum all day,
'But dad a different breed was he;
'They met beneath a cherry tree.
'Though neither parent was consulted,
'They had fun, and I resulted.'

It all put Noah in a fix:
No singletons could join the mix.
'Away!' he said. 'Go to the park!
'No space for you in my new ark.'
So, with a final glance at Noah,
Off he padded, past two boa.
The waters rose, and then abated,
Forty rain-soaked days they'd waited.

With the sun, grass grew in tufts.
Millennia passed, then – new at Crufts –
A cockapoo, a blend of breeds,
Exactly what the dog world needs!

But joy proved brief as, from his seat,
A man had risen to his feet;
An ancient sage with long grey beard,
He cleared his throat. 'It's as I feared,
'I well recall this canine meld,
'I wronged one once; its fate I held
'In both my hands. My conscience since
'Has troubled me… it's made me wince.

'I let him down… abandoned him.'
Which might explain why dogs can swim.

Tim Harrison

Dog

Your fragments of uncommon memory
Conjure a wide open plain
Or perhaps a shaded forest,
Pine-scented, deep and dense
Through which you are running,
tracking, hunting.

The pack sleeps huddled
Bodies close for safety,
Fur bristling against the cold
of the wild night.

Until one day, a hand is outstretched,
Words are murmured
And you move away from your brothers
And closer to the fire.
My dog.

Caroline Brooker

PARMESAN CHEESE

The Path Well Travelled In The Wheelchair Of My Mind

"There will never be arson
In the theatre of my mind,
As the fire curtain
Always comes down."

End. The end. That's all.
All for today, my friend.
As the alopecia of asphalt
Rises up to meet. Wei Chi.

Tao death us do part?
Till the blind beggar sees us
For the first time
At the beginning of Act I?

Are we not then protagonists
Just passing through?
The silent witness to
The maddening landfill

Of consciousness. "What of it?"
Shrieked the municipal gatekeeper,
Seagulls circling his head.
All is dharma.

Michael McFadden

The Abyss

The frames all stand like an army of chrome,
I sip from small cups made of beige plastic,
I live in a prison, not in my home.
A room of strange people, my friends I miss,
Either this or return to my dark cell,
I can't believe my family did this.
Staff watch me in the observation dome,
My nametag sewed in my jumper's fabric,
I live in a prison, not in my home.

Sat on a pad covered in my own piss,
Staff wrap me with talc to disguise the smell,
I can't believe my family did this.
My only treasure, my pink pocket comb,
Robot staff programmed to automatic,
I live in a prison, not in my home.
All I can do for now is reminisce,
Praying today's the day I bid farewell,
I live in a prison, not in my home.
I can't believe my family did this.

Samantha Fyn

Recipe for Harmony

Slice into a prejudice.
Remove the hard stone of fear.
Add the prejudice to a heated pan
And melt in two tablespoons of
Listening and Honesty.
Gently raise the heat until the prejudice
Absorbs the Listening and Honesty
And softens.
Take the jug of Humanity we shared earlier
Pour two cupfuls into the pan
Cook until the mixture bubbles
And smiles form on the surface.
Serve with care while still warm.

Jim Dunk

Spring Clean

I know you don't like poems
But sometimes now and then
I feel the urge to write one
Set down my thoughts on men

I'm hoovering the sitting room
And underneath a chair
I find a fond reminder
Of a man no longer there

We had such fun together
For several years I know
But suddenly there came a time
When I felt he had to go

But when I find the glasses
(the spares he left with me)
I feel a little sorry
That I told the man to flee

Heigh-Ho, that's life.
He may have gone
But memories will linger on

Jenny Richards

In the Rocard Room at the cornerHOUSE on November 16 2018, John Rutter (having regaled us with a couple of Pam Ayres' poems) reads one of his own compositions. It's on **p44**

Time Stands Still

Metal Skin
Nerves so thin
Skin like steel
A cat could peel
Steel my self
Off the shelf
Self destruct
The viaduct
Where I stand
Heart in hand
Stand and stare
Nothing there
Stair to heaven
Not quite eleven
Oh clock
Tick tock
Oh clock
Don't stop
Till seven
My rhythm
Is shot
The race
Is on
To end
This poem
With grace
Save face
Don't breathe
Breathe in
Breathe out
Let go
Don't try
Do try
Face facts
Hard hats
Be strong
Where is
The rhyme
The rhythm
This poem
Had promise
A vision
Of what
Tick tock
Tick tock
Don't stop
Don't stop
Until
Until you
Drop.

Michael McFadden

On the Jetty

What is he thinking, this man alone?
In the grey, shifting mist he is still as stone.
On the jetty – flat planks all damp with slime –
he stands in a gaze: Is it time? Is it time?

Looking out in the dark for a wet-lapped boat
to make its way known with a 'slap slap' sound,
to slide into view through the mirrored river,
carving its wake where the weeds abound?

Time, looking out, for seductive siren
to call from the shore across the lake?
Or mermaid, with flip of her silver tail,
to show him the watery path to take?

Grey is the veil drawn across the skies;
hazy the vision before his eyes;
strange are the sounds of screech and scrape;
deep is the darkness beneath the lake.

Gill Davies

Be Careful What You Wish For

First the eldest child
Squeezed into a box
bedroom
With a tumbling chattering
crowd of tiny siblings
And dreaming of solitude...

Next the lanky anxious
teenager
Crammed into the vast
metropolis of secondary
school
Clattering shoes on endless
corridors
Yells and cries and faces,
faces, everywhere
And dreaming of solitude...

Next the busy mother
surrounded by love
And babies and needy
husband and
puppies and kittens and
hamsters and birds on the
bird table
And dreaming of
solitude…

Now an aged soul reclining
in an empty room
filled with the pain of old
dreams and memories
And hating the solitude!
Be careful what you wish
for…

Alice Maslen

Poppy

In the post arrived today
A single poppy made of clay
Entombed in cardboard coffin white
It's not a thing of beauty

Six red petals fixed athwart
A roughly fashioned iron stalk
By big and ugly nut and bolt
But it has done its duty

It stood through wind and rain and sun
To represent a mother's son
With 888,245 more
All planted in the Tower

Blood swept lands and seas of red
This is what the caption said
Never underestimate
The power of this flower

Jenny Richards

Reflect

That is who I am
Harsh lit
Full front

The image is unforgiving
Not softened.

Flaws and imperfections
Cracks, crevices.

Life etched on skin
Eyes blushed by pollen,
strain and tears.

Stray hairs in irrelevant places
Cracked and bitten lips.

A tiny scar
Memento of something long forgotten

The face launched no ships
But is the front of many slips

Ian Davies

I am the Author

I am the author of my life
I do not halt for your full stops;
Catch my breath at your semi-colons,
So, do not bracket my thoughts
Or contrive to disfigure my words
With your speech marks.
My songs will never feed your metre,
My story never neatly fit
Your paragraphs.
My words, my children
Will run wild and free,
Happy in the jungle-jumble
Of my verse,
Streetwise in the concrete
Of my poetry.
I am the author of my life
And I will not go to my grave
Afraid of ghost writers.

Jim Dunk

Intruder in my House

Hello, did we pass in the hall?
Silly I know, but I don't actually recall
my memory isn't always at its best,
this time of night
would you mind
answering my question,
to give my heart a rest?
I do really thank you for dropping by
Ring next time, send a postcard,
it would be such a pity to miss you
yes, I'm trying not to cry

How can you refuse to go?
It's hard stifling my fear
as it's hiding behind me,
knees trembling,
hoping no one will hear.
Don't you see,
I'm actually frightened now
Stop clowning around,
OK if you wish,
I won't make a sound

You're holding my arms very tight
Is it necessary to use all your might?

Look at me, yes, short and slight
My eyes are the same colour as yours
I'm sure we must be related
somewhere along the line
I beg you, isn't there a link
somewhere in time,
Thank God.... a knock at the door.
I scream.
My brother, the hero, rushes in
in the nick of time.

Paula Scott

Science

Oh… she's so good at art
Just like her mother
So creative
What fun we had in those formative years
Making and painting, snipping and sewing
Pre-school, infants, juniors
I could always help
I had the knowledge, the skills
…and then
Science!

It drew you in and others made a path for
you to follow
Away from the familiar to the unknown
Out into the stratosphere you flew
Arms outstretched so eager to embrace
new encounters.
No more making, painting, snipping and
sewing
I stood close by and listened with awe
As you talked about the cortex,
Neurons, synapses and more.

And yet as the years went by
You took me with you
Showed me pictures of brains I never
would have seen
And we shared a world of microscopic
beauty.

I can breathe again
Maybe no more making, painting snipping
and sewing
As our lives have moved to another sphere
And yet our worlds will always co-exist
In a beautiful swirling, cosmic bliss.

Nicky Newberry

Rhythm of Acceptance

"The wheels have come off!"
Said Vincent Van Gogh.
Let's paint them bright red
And take them to bed.

The truckload of junk
I keep under my bunk:
The baggage I choose
For I cannot lose

The memories of old
All outlined in bold,
Fields of vermilion:
Monet's oblivion.

Where should I go
When the paintbrush won't
flow?
For lack of a rhythm
There opens a schism

In this place of drought
I struggle with doubt:
Try as I might
To let in the light

The dark closes in:
The shadows, they grin
As if to exalt
"You've ground to a halt!"

The wheels are all broken,
The rhythm has spoken.
The sky in cerise
A vision, of peace

Michael McFadden

What Changed?

To have and to hold forever we'd be,
The words we declared on our special day,
If I love him more maybe he'll love me.
The love he showed to his newly wed bride,
The fondness, his eyes really did show,
The pain he rages burns to my inside.
When did this change my memory does plea,
I hope, I believe, it won't stay this way.
If I love him more maybe he'll love me.
The hurt throbbing as I questioned and cried,
Emotions he played so scornful and so slow,
The pain he rages burns to my inside.
His fists pummel down on a feeble me,
When did I become his drunken live prey?
If I love him more maybe he'll love me.
Now all I have are the bruises to hide,
I keep pretending but really I know,
If I love him more maybe he'll love me.
The pain he rages burns to my inside.

Samantha Fyn

March Sonnet

March 10th is Mother's Day
I think of those who've gone away
My mother first, so very dear
Then grandmothers, both no longer here
And thus I slip down history's pain
Considering how each mother's pain
Produced a family line which meant
That I can sit here quite content
And think about what was and is
And what's to come and whether 'tis
Assured that further down the line
Another may twist the strand of time
To think back through maternal ties
While pondering complicated lives
A link is forged which can't be broken
Twixt past and future yet unspoken

Jenny Richards

DINING ON CARR'S AND RYVITA SNACKS

Drive

So, shall we go away? Grab the last stab at summer,
the sunlight bright through turning trees?
Find a quiet place near glistening sea: a little hotel or B&B,
a bed, a view, and you and me?

Shall we find somewhere new with a pin on a map?
Through a wall of trees, a leafy lane,
leave the traffic and fumes, the M25
to disappear in a distance of dust... and drive.

Sand under our feet or a neat little tearoom
with cakes, clotted cream, steamy panes from the heat,
nothing fancy. A change from the grey winter rain
waiting just round the corner from our concrete street.

A few pounds from the bank, some clean knickers and hankies,
a tank full of petrol – let's go!
while the sun paints the shade to a kindlier hue.
Let's run to the sea for a different view.

Gill Davies

Ariadne

Sometimes, as night fell and the smell of the olive groves
Drifted across the courtyards and colonnades of the palace,
I would leave the warm safety of my room
And silently descend the cool stone steps
To the mouth of the labyrinth,
Taking into my nostrils the animal scent
Of my poor, misshapen half-brother.

From deep within the maze would come
A low bellowing, a heart-breaking cry
Of a monster trapped and destined
To live out his days in fetid darkness.
And yet, I envied him his solitude.

I wanted for nothing except nothingness itself;
The cool, calm silence of being alone.
But my life was sunlit,
Bright with attendants and servants,
Advisors and siblings swarming,
A constant bee-like buzz
That refused to be still.

Feasts of fish and flesh, rosemary and honey,
Almonds and bread and figs and wine.
Frescoed walls, fountains and dancing.

Mild, wet winters and hot, dry summers.
While high up in the White Mountains,
Snow and silence.

I suppose he was handsome
In an obvious, Athenian way:
All teeth and hair and sun-bronzed skin.
Legend will say I fell in love with him.

My father, the King,
A powerful man, unused to being disobeyed,
Would not take kindly to his daughter
Aiding the enemy with her ball of string.

With my misguided attempt to help this hero,
I have tethered myself to him,
To a repeated life of palaces and people.
I look down at the skein in my hands,
The finest of threads which binds me
Tighter than any chain.
From my robes, I remove
A tiny pair of golden shears.
Snip.
And away I walk
Towards the White Mountains.

Caroline Brooker

Along the Tracks

Along the tracks
No looking back
Pulling me forward
Urging me on
Taking me someplace

I like the motion
Away from commotion
Drifting from place to place
In my mind
Swaying and gliding
Chasing the wind

Travelling internally
Arriving externally
Along the tracks
Over the tracks
Taking me here
Taking me there
Time to think
Time to stare

Going over the tracks
Over the memories
Life is warm
Life is good
Taking me here
Taking me there…
Taking me home

Nicky Newberry

Treasure

Drive them to a mountain stream
Drive them to a rocky beach
Bring them to a mountain path
Bring them to a white sandy beach.

Give them thirteen hours
in the back seat of the car
with a book, a pillow and a toy monkey.
Give them a steamed-up window
to play noughts and crosses on.

Bring them a two-hour traffic jam
diverted at midnight on the M6.

Show them a couple of sheep in a field.
Show them a sparrow,
a shipwreck and a standing stone.

Bring them biscuits for breakfast,
hot chocolate for lunch
and chips for dinner.

Show them grey skies
and a thin seam of silver light
stretching over a Loch.

Show them swallows at dusk.
There are eagles in the hills.
Make them sleep in a broken tent
with three inches of water
at the bottom.

Tell them this is a holiday
Leave them on a rain-drenched beach
for two hours
until their hands and toes turn blue.

Tell them it will be better tomorrow.

Buy them fishing nets and a football.
Make them set up camp
three times in four days
in hard wind-driven rain.

Don't let them see you cry.

Show them flowering Lichen
Orchids, Rock Rose,
Cotton Grass and Heather.
Let them drink mountain water
from Sphagnum Moss.

Show them a rainbow
stretched across the island
we are leaving.
And watch a light
shine from their wind-weary faces.
And watch their smiles lift you higher
than all the rain-grey clouds.

David Loffman

South

Look at the photograph.
Tell me what you see.
Four fur-wrapped figures, faces indistinct.
Flag flying from a makeshift flagpole.
From this blurred image you cannot imagine
The biting cold and the noise of the wind,
The whiteness of the landscape,
So harsh you screw up your eyes against the
glare.

Chosen for our loyalty, our intelligence,
our bravery,
We sailed from Greenland and life on board
was good.
We were well fed, we found companionship
And together we weathered fierce storms,
Large groups pressed together against the
pitch and roll of the ship,
The swell and spray of the waves.

On landing, the shock of work after months
of rest
Meant our ship-softened feet bled for days
Until the hardening of the skin.
Sledges were filled with supplies.
We pulled these to base camp,
And there we slept fitfully,
Curled up tightly together in icy beds,
Shallow canvas-roofed snow trenches.

During our danger-shadowed journey,
Comrades froze to death in their sleep
And, as we crossed the crevassed uncertainty
of ice,
Snow gave way under our feet to reveal
An abyss of terrible, plunging darkness.

For days on end, we heaved our way up the
giant glacier,
Bellies scraping the snow,
The only sounds to reach our ears -
Panting breath,
Creaking sledge.

As we made camp
Another sound assaulted our ears.
We started as the first shot rang out.
And when the shooting was over
A deafening silence, louder than any gunfire.

Days bled into each other
We struggled on, hunger stalking every step,
The unremitting wind and whiteness sapping
our strength
Until the reaction of our leader told us we had
reached our goal
A spot that, to my jaded eyes
Looked no different from the many miles
already covered.

Readings, measurements and photographs
were taken.
Exhausted, I could only sit and watch the
activity.
And when I saw my master approaching,
Sad smile on his face, pistol in hand
I know that I too had reached the end of my
journey.

Now look at the photograph.
Tell me what you see.
Four men, a flag and, sitting to one side and
staring straight at the camera,
A dog,
Fur ruffled by the cold hand of the wind
Image forever frozen in time.

My name is Helge.
I sailed on the Fram
I reached the South Pole.
And now, as I run with my brothers
Across ice plains of eternity,
We howl our proud Norse names to the wind.

Caroline Brooker

A Good Beach

Sand yachts skitter up and down
Like insects, clattering dragonfly wings.
The sand is flat; a good surface for wheels,
Smooth, no rocks to impede progress.
The yachts race around one another joyfully,
The wind whipping their sky blue sails.
They celebrate the good beach with its perfect sand.
The surf is gentle, a good beach for paddling,
It has a shallow, sloping shoreline, good for wading ashore.
The pebbles on the beach are smooth and are the colour of eggs.
They are sometimes stained with rust, like blood.
Where the beach ends, the land rises up
In mangled, grassy tussocks.
A military band can be heard faintly from the cemetery,
The sound caught by the wind and
Tossed over the sand.
A small group of old men look out over the beach, remembering.
"Férocité est de dormir sur le sable."
The sand is no longer flat.
The shells are made of brass and cleave the air.
The wind and waves cannot be heard over the scream of artillery and the cries of the dying.
The waves never stop.
The wind never stops.
The sand re-forms smooth and clean with each tide.
This is Omaha.

Hilary Walker

CAERPHILLY ON WHEATEN

So Let Us Shine

Ann
Lowes

Guiding latecomers with her trusty torch as
Front of House
Ann was a regular shining light at the
cornerHOUSE.
Though I'm tempted to say she was a 'leading
light',
She was a retiring sort, who might have said that
wasn't right.
She would come forward to help out if she
thought she ought
But it was never the limelight that she sought.
Still her face often lit up with a rather cheeky grin
And, even without a torch, she shone from
within.

I'll miss you, Ann; I could tell you
a joke and you got it.
And, if there was ever a funny
side, then you were quick to spot
it.
I don't think you'd want a fuss now
your torch has been extinguished
Or for us to go overboard and
celebrate you as 'someone quite
distinguished'.
A shining example to us all, never
a whited sepulchre,
I'm sure I'm not the only one who's
really going to miss her.
With that touch of roguish
humour, a ready smile on her face,
I can, in all honesty, say:
Ann always brightened up the
place.

Valerie Nunn

(*In memory of Ann Lowes,
April 30 1943-August 8 2018*)

Moving Away

And each slow dusk a drawing-down
of blinds
You'd have recognised that line
After all, poetry was your thing
Your father's gift, and one of your loves,
like the husband and sons
whom you watched with tender regret
as they chose music over words.

A drawing-down it was,
your pilot gone, flown before you,
leaving the house to its own slow dusk;
imperceptible at first, but as months
turned to years
the shades lengthened over the
windows,
and the door of each room of the mind
began to close
at the touch of time's gentle, cruel hand.
A familiar name forgotten,
an inexplicable confusion
about the way home that you'd taken a
thousand times
And a creeping dread.
Then, quite suddenly, the door to
independence slammed shut,
a fresh bereavement
leaving you rootless and afraid.

And, more slowly,
other doors swung to:
the one leading to what happened
yesterday,
and the next, that sealed up eternally
the comfortable parlour of distant
memory.
But how the hinges groaned in pain
at the cruel pressure that twisted them
round!
Finally you were left standing in the
hallway:
the corridor of the continuous present,

emerging from the shadows and leading
nowhere.
Some could visit you there, shining
fleeting torches of love.

You escaped under cover of darkness
ceasing not upon the midnight
but one winter morning early,
an unfamiliar hand, not mine,
holding yours
as you turned the final key,
heading for the light.
The house, once so bright with the
beauty of life,
lies abandoned
but there is one door that remains open
for ever.

Simon Hancock

*(In memory of his mother, Marjorie,
who died on January 16 2016, aged 93)*

A Brief History of Hawking

I sit alone and marvel
At Stephen Hawking's life
The sums, the calculations
And why he left his wife

That so much could be going
on
Inside that tilted head
The secrets of creation
A science A-Z

His death has got me
wondering
As winter turns to spring
Would he have been as
world-renowned
Without that voicebox thing?

Say he'd just been a lecturer
On two feet, firm and strong
Would he just be a scientist?
Part of an endless throng?

The wheelchair was his
trademark
The voice his trademark too
A truly stellar genius
A wonder to review

Tim Harrison

Whitton

She had made a million cups of
tea
in her 84 years, but now
she couldn't remember how

Muttering endlessly about the
weather
she proudly presented me a mug
of warm milk, the key ingredient
missing

I smiled politely before pouring
it onto the pansies, Whitton

once famed for its market gardens;
roses, narcissi and fruit orchards,
now a grey suburb, on the edge
of nowhere, rumbling under
flightpath,
the old village consumed
by that ever-expanding black hole,
London

Oh, the sadness of the sun
setting over West London,
casting long shadow over
patches of forgotten fields
where horses still roam

Rob Tuck

True to a Class, Darkly

"Can any age wear these?" she said
Her voice betrayed a social dread
She was of a generation
Untrained in such interrogation.
The shop assistant, knowing,
smiled
She fawned without, within,
reviled.
"Why, yes. All ages wear them, pet.
You're not so old that you can't, yet".
Considering the judicious lie,
The lady looked, released a sigh
What now? 'To buy or not to buy'
A question just as full of terror
As Hamlet's, and as prone to error.
If she should make the wrong
decision,
Expose herself to friends' derision
"Who does she think she is?" they'd
mumble
Her self-regard they'd quickly
humble.
A woman of a certain age
In shoes like that, incites to rage
The harpy crew with lemon lips
And armour plate of kirby grips.
I saw her crumble, shrink inside
Embarrassed that she'd even tried
To make her mark upon life's street,
With youthful shoes upon her feet.
And there, within the shoe shop
glass,
She saw her feet, her age, her class,
Gave up her struggle and grew old
Gathered her coat 'gainst sudden
cold
Found her pride quite indefensible
And chose some shoes that were
…just sensible.

Jim Dunk

On Reflection

"Who's that old dear – what's her
game then?"
A friend told me his granny once
asked.
Though her puzzlement stayed just
the same when
The mystery 'old dear' was
unmasked.

"That's you, Gran, that is – in
reflection;
"In the mirror they've put in the lift."
The old lady can't see the
connection;
Only asks: "Can't you tell 'er to
shift?"

Friends tell me I'm no adolescent,
Though I feel young and vibrant
inside.
The barometer points to
senescent –
Not the first time, I think, that it's
lied.

I often catch a glimpse of some
youngster
And for a moment think that I've
seen
Some long lost pal still amongst us –
If that old friend had stayed
seventeen.

And so, now that I've got my bus
pass,
All mirrors from the house I shall
ban.
Cos, whenever I look in the glass,
These days all I can see is my gran.

Valerie Nunn

The Mother's Gift

In the winter my baby child was born,
Perfect was my son as I held him near,
Without him, my weakened heart would be torn,
And our bond grew stronger year upon year,
The milestones, birthdays, memories so dear.
I wish I could lock in a box and seal,
No more does he need his Mama it's clear,
The pain, it hurts so much, only I feel,
But soon I know my feelings they will heal,
I nurtured you well, grew you to be free,
A young, good man now, with life you can deal,
Adult years unlocked, handing you the key.
I look at you now, a fresh set of eyes,
I know no one can break mother-son ties.

Samantha Fyn

Music and Movement

"Now can you be a pony? Lift your feet
and prance!"
As twenty-five small children clattered
round the hall,
One little would-be pony was not
impressed at all;
She'd have cluttered off out of there,
given half a chance.

A lady's sing-song voice was asking:
"Can you be a tree?"
And fifty small, galumphing feet
staggered to a stop;
Fifty whitewashed plimsolls were
caught on the hop,
Cos every skule boy knows a tree stands
still as still can be.

"Now stretch those arms up, up, up and
reach for the sky!"
Fifty hands went up, up, up – oh, ever
so high.
We reached for the sky, as if in a raid –
Or twenty-five beanpoles lined up on
parade.

Straight as an arrow, with never a
quiver,
Each child strained every nerve to stand
and deliver.
Not one of these trees let a branch
gently sway,
The music had stopped now, we weren't
meant to sashay.

This wasn't what they'd promised on my
first day at school.
"There will be dancing," they had said.
And I believed them – what a fool!
But there was only cantering and then
some standing still,
And people saying silly things like
"Now can you be a house?"

Would Alicia Markova pretend to be a
house?
Did the Ballets Russes ever ape a
stock-still tree?
I bet they never did, so why would you
ask me?
Don't tell me to be "a statue" or "quiet as
a mouse!"

A tree is not a lifeless thing, not stolid
or unmoving.
However high it climbs, however great
its girth,
However firmly tethered its ancient
roots are to the earth,
A breath of wind can move it and make
the canopy sing.

So let your trees go twirling, I really
love to twirl.
It's poetry in motion, the ultimate in
swirl.
And when there's music, I want
movement, says
That once obediently still, but *furious*
little girl.

Valerie Nunn

MASCARPONE or ROULÉ

An Uphill Struggle

I find it difficult to cope
With Sainsbury's being on a slope
Fruit and veg is run-of-mill
But other things are up the hill

I worry that one careless day
My set of wheels might roll away
On Saturday I nearly died
While trolleying up that mountainside

Has Surbiton another shop
With such a noticeable drop?
For any time I'm running late
I have to face that one-in-eight

I dream some day I'll reach the wine
But it is high up the incline
So steep you feel the need for crampons
When you're buying packs of thingamies

Morris Thain

Dish me a Dollop of Poetry

Dish me a dollop of poetry,
with a sprinkling of rhyme on the side.
Pour me a soupcon of balladry,
With a small pinch of passion applied.
I don't care if it has perfect metre,
If it's true to a well-chosen form
If the stanzas are tidy and neater,
And the couplets are clipped to
conform.
Let the words stand free of convention
Let them settle wherever they fall
Let them dance and cavort on the page
I say,
Let them challenge and break every
rule.
So dish me a dollop of poetry
A splash or a splodge or a splatter
As long as the meaning can move me,
The rest of it just doesn't matter.

Della Reynolds

Work

Sometimes I rush home from work
only to sit in silence, wondering why

I rushed home from work

Rob Tuck

Text

The cool night air feels good
At the bus stop I
write a text but
don't send it

I dwell on the words
They look stupid
Just squiggles
I am drunk

A text saved as draft is worth 100 sent

Rob Tuck

Dinner Time

On the island of Mauritius
A crew of hungry sailors
Sit, pounding on the table.

Why are we waiting
Oh, why are we waiting?

The sweating cook sticks
His head through the hatch.
Shouts angrily
Any minute now!

What is it?
A brave old salt demands.

A roast,
The chef proclaims.

A roast what?
A chorus of hungry voices demands.

Dodo.

As one
the crew groans and shouts.
Not again!

Don't worry,
Says cook.

It's the last one.

Ian Davies

LYMESWOLD

A Study in Blue

Humpty Dumpty had a way with words
They meant whatever he wanted them to.
But the most versatile word that he used
Was that maverick colour we called Blue.

Blue is so sad in my mood, on a bruise.
The stern attitude in a steely blue stare
Which brooks no argument and cautions 'Beware'
Those dancing feet wore blue suede shoes,
That soulful music was singing the blues.

The colour of oceans can be happy, or warn
Of a strong tempest coming sometime this morn.
A welding torch when hot is blue
Though Arctic cold comes in that hue
My fingers and toes in Winter are too.

The temper of steel when given an edge
And quality tools for cutting a hedge.
The assuring tones of uniformed police
Firemen and nurses are welcomed and nice.

But happy is blue in the colour of your eyes
And happy again in soft Summer skies

Vera Lynn sang of birds over Dover
And woods of bluebells and fields of clover.
Some stories and jokes are so described too.
But none of the phrases I use are blue.

John Rutter